POETRY AND THE
EDUCATION OF COMPASSION

PROFESSOR PATRICK PIETRONI

FRESCO BOOKS

CONTENTS

This book is dedicated to Maurice Irfan Coles, CEO and founder of The CoED Foundation, who has done the most work on insuring that compassion has a central place in the educational curriculum.

SOUNDS, MUSIC, GAZING AND TOUCH

They say you learn it from your mother
That she will always be there for you
You, of course, know nothing of this
For your brain is not formed
For you to receive.

Yet, somehow you do know
You know in your body first
Then in your mind
At about six weeks you learn
To smile and to gurgle
No language yet, but you
Listen, look and feel
To sounds, to music, to gazing and touch
(yes and yes again).

You grow up, you marry
You have your own children
Don't preach to them.

You cannot teach what you have learnt
Remember what your mother did.

Sounds, music, gazing and touch
That is all you need
To help your children and yourself
To become compassionate
To others
It is sometimes called love.

Patrick Pietroni [1]

INTRODUCTION

In the first volume of this series, *The Poetry of Compassion*, I introduced the concept of compassion and how Charles Darwin's research suggests that the human species has evolved to behave compassionately, or at least, that we have the capacity to do so. In the *Descent of Man,* he wrote:

> *"We are … impelled to relieve the sufferings of another, in order that our own painful feelings may be at the same time relieved. In like manner we are led to participate in the pleasures of others."* [2]

Recent discoveries in neuroscience and neuro-imaging support this biological basis for compassion, but it was Darwin who originally argued that,

> *"[T]hose communities which contained the greatest number of the most sympathetic members would flourish best, and rear the greatest number of offspring".* [3]

I then outlined using selected poems how the following concepts of compassion could be understood:

Proximal compassion
Distal compassion
Global compassion
Self-compassion
Compassion fatigue

In the second volume, *Poetry and the Science of Compassion*, again using selected poems, I outlined how science, especially how neuroscience has allowed us to understand the biological, chemical, and physical basis of the nature of compassion.

I described how each of the following chemicals (neurotransmitters) has both a specific and general effect on our physical, emotional, and cognitive experience in relation to compassion: dopamine, serotonin, endorphin, oxytocin, and cortisol.

In the third volume, *The Poetry of Global Compassion*, using Ronald Higgin's approach, again with selected poems, I summarised the seven enemies he outlined in his book (*The Seventh Enemy*[4]). These include:

1. World population growth
2. Food shortage and food facts
3. Alarming environmental degradation
4. Depletion of earth's natural resources
5. The nuclear threat
6. Science and technology galloping at a speed beyond human control
7. The human factor

I ended this third volume by quoting a thirteenth-century Persian poet – Rumi.

ALL RIVERS AT ONCE
(extract)

What is the body? Endurance.
What is love? Gratitude.
What is hidden in our chests? Laughter.
What else? Compassion.

Jalal ad-Din Muhammad Rumi [5]

In this fourth volume, I tackle the challenges posed by the questions: 1) Can we create an educational system that can include a compassionate curriculum? 2) What does such a curriculum include and how should it be delivered?

Since Karen Armstrong's TED talk on compassion in 2008[6] there has been an ever-increasing academic interest in the concept of compassion, and much research and experimentation has been undertaken that will form much of the content of this volume. It would, however, be remiss of us if we assumed many others well before us had not also tackled this challenge.

Experimental educational approaches such as that begun by Alexander Neill at Summerhill School (1921, Suffolk, UK)[7] proved very popular also in the United States, as was the Montessori Method[8] founded by Dr. Maria Montessori, the Italian paediatrician/psychiatrist. A more recent experiment, The Open University,[9] focussing on non-residential education, was launched in the UK in 1969. Although no longer as creative as its first three decades, it nevertheless gave many adults the opportunity to return to a learning environment, allowing them to meet their own educational needs as identified by themselves. There are several similarities between these educational approaches embedded in the philosophy of these experiments. These included "freedom, not license", "choice and self-direction", and "a focus on collaboration and not competition". The combination of independent, small groups, and whole group learning helps to stimulate both collaboration, leadership, and life-long learning. It is clear that the emphasis is as much on the "teaching method" as it is on the curriculum content.

I have chosen to explore in greater detail how the compassionate development of a child can be encouraged or not, as he/she journeys through their "three score years and ten". This must now be changed to "four score years and ten" as many of us live past our 90s.

This first poem, by who else, but Shakespeare, will form part of our guide and I have taken the liberty of adding to the "Seven Ages of Man" this soliloquy from "As You Like It," Act II, Scene VII:

ALL THE WORLD'S A STAGE

All the world's a stage,
And all the men and women merely players;
They have their exits and their entrances;
And one man in his time plays many parts,
His acts being seven ages. At first the infant,
Mewling and puking in the nurse's arms;
And then the whining school-boy, with his satchel
And shining morning face, creeping like snail
Unwillingly to school. And then the lover,
Sighing like furnace, with a woeful ballad
Made to his mistress' eyebrow. Then a soldier,
Full of strange oaths, and bearded like the pard,
Jealous in honour, sudden and quick in quarrel,
Seeking the bubble reputation
Even in the cannon's mouth. And then the justice,
In fair round belly with good capon lin'd,
With eyes severe and beard of formal cut,
Full of wise saws and modern instances;
And so he plays his part. The sixth age shifts
Into the lean and slipper'd pantaloon,
With spectacles on nose and pouch on side;
His youthful hose, well sav'd, a world too wide
For his shrunk shank; and his big manly voice,
Turning again toward childish treble, pipes
And whistles in his sound. Last scene of all,
That ends this strange eventful history,
Is second childishness and mere oblivion;
Sans teeth, sans eyes, sans taste, sans everything.

William Shakespeare [10]

I have chosen to focus on the following stages and have identified some of the important existing work regarding the "compassionate curriculum" linked to each:

0-5 years	*Attachment Theory* – John Bowlby [11]
	Attachment and Mirror Neurons – several authors
5-17 years	*Towards the Compassionate School* – Maurice Irfan Coles. [12]
	Teaching with Heart – Sam Intrator and Megan Scribner [13]
17-30 years	*The Compassionate University* – Kathryn Waddington[14]
30-65 years	*Fit for Purpose* – many authors
	Life-long Learning
65-90 years	*Education in the Third Age* – many authors

The Use of Poetry

I have selected a poem that says something important about each of the world's seven ages identified by Shakespeare's famous soliloquy, "All the World's a Stage".

Poetry is of particular importance in our educational system, both formal and informal.

Elena Aguilar, writing for the George Lucas Educational Foundation[15] in 2013 explored the five reasons why we need poetry in schools:

1. *Poetry helps us know each other and build community. Poetry allows children to put language to use to make it serve a deep internal purpose and to break rules along the way.*
2. *When read aloud, poetry is rhythm and music and sounds and beats – babies and preschoolers included may not understand all the words or meaning, but they will feel the rhythms, get curious about what the sounds mean and perhaps want to create their own.*
3. *Poetry opens venues for speaking and listening and motivates reluctant writers.*
4. *Because poems defy rules, they can be made accessible to English language learners and allow them to find ways of expressing their voices whilst being limited in their vocabulary.*
5. *Poetry fosters social and emotional learning. A well-crafted phrase or two in a poem can help us see an experience in an entirely new way.*

Emily Southerton (Director of The Poet Warriors Project [16]) helps children write and publish poetry on tough issues they face, such as poverty, gangs and peer pressure. She writes:

Poetry ignites students to think about what it's like to share their opinion, be heard, and make a difference in their world. Students can let go of traditional writing rules with poetry. I tell the kids the most important thing about poetry is that people feel differently after reading it. [17]

0–5 Years

I NEVER KNEW

I never knew I could love so much,
until the day I felt your touch.

I softly kissed your tiny cheek,
and from under your lashes I saw you peek.

Your beautiful eyes so small and blue,
my sweet little baby just brand new.

I cannot wait to watch you grow,
from your little head to your tiny toes.

My daughter, my love, my little joy,
my little angel, my baby doll toy.

I promise to love you with all my heart.
I'm here for you from the very start.

I'll comfort you when you cry,
I'll answer true when you ask me, "Why?"

While you grow, be sweet and kind,
and show all others how much you shine.

Martha L. Sheridan[18]

"Give me the first five years of a child's life and I will give you a saint or a devil"[19] often attributed to Voltaire, who himself attributed it to Ignatus of Loyola, and taken up by the Roman Catholic Church as its own dictum. There is now much scientific and research study that supports the statement.

At birth a baby has more than 100 billion nerve cells and brain growth and development and by age 5 has reached 85% of the total brain growth. Learning requires the nerve cells or neurons to be connected together.

In the last decade or so with the advent of neuro-imaging we can observe how the mother's behaviour towards the baby's activities is of immense importance. The following three descriptions will help to explain how the capacity for empathetic responses (compassion) are developed and can be encouraged, making the mother or mother-substitute the earliest teacher/trainer/instructor for the baby's subsequent growth.

Attachment Theory

Developed by John Bowlby (1907-1990) a psychoanalyst, psychologist, and psychiatrist working at the Tavistock Clinic in London, Bowlby began his life work before the Second World War. His first responsibility was working with young boys who were separated from their families for petty crimes. Bowlby's work differs in one central and crucial way from the work of many analytic theorists. It is not based solely on the retrospective formulation of clinical data but on observational data gathered in many different situations outside the analyst's room. It draws on observation of animal behaviour and animal experiments as well as meticulously observed human encounters. Bowlby's original observations have now been repeated across cultures, and across species. He published his main work in the three-volume work *Attachment, Separation and Loss*,[20] and his later books included *The Making and Breaking of Affectional Bonds* (1979)[21] and *A Secure Base: Clinical Application of Attachment Theory* (1988)[22]. Just before he died, he finished a biography of Charles Darwin, which is an essay in applied Bowlbyism.[23] A quote from 1968 illustrates the simplicity and common sense nature of the man:

> *... there are few blows to human spirit so great as the loss of someone near and dear. Traditional wisdom knows that we can be crushed by grief and die of a broken heart, and also that a jilted lover is apt to do things that are foolish and dangerous to himself and others. It knows too that neither love nor grief is felt for just any other human being, but only for one, or a few, particular and individual human beings. The core of what I term an 'affectional bond' is the attraction that one individual has for another individual.* [24]

In brief, Bowlby argues:

> *Attachment behaviour, it is argued, is a form of instinctive behaviour that develops in humans, as in other mammals, during infancy, and has as its aim or goal proximity to a mother-figure. The function of attachment behaviour, it is suggested is protection from predators. Whilst attachment behaviour is shown especially strongly during childhood when it is directed towards parent figures, it none the less continues to be active during adult life when it is usually*

directed towards some active and dominant figure, often a relative but sometimes an employer or some elder of the community. Attachment behaviour, the theory emphasizes, is elicited whenever a person (child or adult) is sick or in trouble, and is elicited at high intensity when he is frightened or when the attachment figure cannot be found. Because, in the light of this theory, attachment behaviour is regarded as a normal and healthy part of man's instinctive makeup, it is held to be misleading to term it 'regressive' or childish when seen in older child or adult. For this reason, too the term 'dependency' is regarded as leading to a seriously mistaken perspective: for in everyday speech to describe someone as dependent cannot help carrying with it overtones of criticism. By contrast, to describe someone as attached carries with it a positive evaluation.[25]

Mirror Neurons and Attachment

As the result of brain imaging technology, it has been possible to observe which parts of the brain ìlight upî when we are reading, having a conversation, or listening to music. Studies of mothers breast feeding their babies have shown when the mother "mirrors" the baby's face with smiles or gurgles, similar to those the baby makes, i.e. mirrors the baby's behaviour, there exists "attunement between them". The hypothesis being that brain scans of both mother and baby would demonstrate the same part of the brain would light up. When the mother is inattentive or non-observing of the babies face, i.e. non-attuned, different parts of the brain light up.

During the first few years of life, the ability of a mother to be attuned to the needs of her infant is crucial to their development. This attunement is important to a child's ability to learn to regulate their nervous system and deal with distressing events. When a mother consistently fails to be attuned, different types of insecure attachment result. One could say that a mother's attunement is the building block to how one learns to be connected to others, build relationships, and feel safe in the world.

A definition of attunement:

... is a kinesthetic and emotional sensing of the other— knowing their rhythm, affect, and experience by metaphorically being in their skin, and going beyond empathy to create a two-person experience of unbroken feeling connectedness by providing a reciprocal affect and/or resonating response [26]

Attunement allows us to respond with compassion to another's experience.

In summary, I would add that we now have the anthropological, the psychological (Bowlby), the biological (Lorenz), the scientific (neuro imagining) evidence to support the view that:

a. The first five years of an infant's experience are of major importance in the learning he/she achieves
b. This learning involves both cognitive (languages/and emotional/relational skills)
c. The "mother" or substitute mother is the critical input into what the child learns, especially in the emotional education between five and seventeen/eighteen years of age.

d. Mindfulness training and helping the child to breathe slowly and deeply is now a much more common activity that teachers (and the research) have shown to have marked benefits that can be achieved.

5–17 YEARS

IF

If you can keep your head when all about you
    Are losing theirs and blaming it on you,
If you can trust yourself when all men doubt you,
    But make allowance for their doubting too;
If you can wait and not be tired by waiting,
    Or being lied about, don't deal in lies,
Or being hated, don't give way to hating,
    And yet don't look too good, nor talk too wise:

If you can dream—and not make dreams your master;
    If you can think—and not make thoughts your aim;
If you can meet with Triumph and Disaster
    And treat those two impostors just the same;
If you can bear to hear the truth you've spoken
    Twisted by knaves to make a trap for fools,
Or watch the things you gave your life to, broken,
    And stoop and build 'em up with worn-out tools:

If you can make one heap of all your winnings
    And risk it on one turn of pitch-and-toss,
And lose, and start again at your beginnings
    And never breathe a word about your loss;
If you can force your heart and nerve and sinew
    To serve your turn long after they are gone,
And so hold on when there is nothing in you
    Except the Will which says to them: 'Hold on!'

If you can talk with crowds and keep your virtue,
    Or walk with Kings—nor lose the common touch,
If neither foes nor loving friends can hurt you,
    If all men count with you, but none too much;
If you can fill the unforgiving minute
    With sixty seconds' worth of distance run,
Yours is the Earth and everything that's in it,
    And—which is more—you'll be a Man, my son!

Rudyard Kipling [27]

My friend and colleague, Maurice Irfan Coles, who sadly succumbed to Covid-19 in April 2020 as this book was going to press, has led the field in the UK and travelled over the globe giving seminars and workshops on his life's work of working towards the compassionate school (the title of his first book on this subject [28]). Together with colleagues he has assembled the why, the what, and the how to ensure the Golden Rule (treat others as you wish to be treated) can become a Golden Thread throughout a child's educational journey from the years of five to seventeen, ensuring that, unlike Shakespeare's description, this boy/girl is not the whining school-boy, with his satchel and shining morning face, creeping like snail unwillingly to school.

Compassion is one of the oldest, simplest and most intuitive forces in human history. It is a universal, timeless, and radical concept that does not depend on any one culture. It can give our lives a sense of meaning and purpose, and contribute to our health and wellbeing. Although we are wired for compassion, our old brain psychologies – the cortisone-driven fear and flight mode – serve to undermine our better instinct. The best of world religions, the ancient contemplative traditions and contemporary secular neuroscience, psychology and mindfulness provide significant supportive signposts in our journey towards the compassionate school. Access for young people, however, depends on the context of their upbringing, whom they meet and what they read and watch. What is urgently required is an education system that teaches about compassion, teaches compassionately, and encourages 'acts of love': a system, in short, that has collaboration and service as its highest ideals.

On one level this looks like the agenda from hell – another series of impossible burdens that, once again, principals, teachers, support staff and governors are asked to shoulder with no extra resources and no overall direction. But, on another, it looks manageable. Yes, it is a big agenda, but it is something schools are already doing in many ways. The trick is to begin to make the compassionate journey <u>intentional</u>, to make it <u>the key organizing principle of school life</u>. It will, or course, need to be achieved on an incremental basis with each area of school life scrutinized through the prism of compassion.

Education and society's tectonic plates are shifting. They are moving away from a narrow attainment-based, individual-istic, consumerist focus toward something that stresses collab-oration and service. Let us not, however, make our claims too extravagant. Compassion – and compassionate education – is not a magic wand, a panacea for all the world's ills. No such thing exists. It can, however, be the magic wardrobe through which young people can walk to find their own solutions to the problematic legacies we are leaving behind.

Educators have a key role, if not <u>the</u> key role in helping to bring this about. This book tries to provide a theoretical underpinning and practical supportive steps. But how do we know if we have achieved it? What would a compassion-ate school actually look like?

A compassionate school would exhibit all or some of the following characteristics. It would:

- *have compassion as its key ongoing organizing principle, so that it permeates everything the school does*
- *ensure compassion infuses and enthuses its curriculum content and curricular processes*
- *ensure compassion forms the bedrock of initial teacher and continuing professional development*
- *have signed the Charter for Compassion with the Golden Rule as its heart, and with the Golden Thread pulsating through its arteries*
- *use the taxonomy of compassion 'acts for love', as a key vehicle for both values transmission and as an audit tool*
- *have a complete workforce, including school governors and managers, who articulate the vision and live its principles*
- *have leaders, staff, parents and carers who model these values*
- *have a pupil population who aspires to these ideals, which will be clearly visible, both in their behaviours and in how they treat each other and adults in the school and beyond*
- *employ pupil, staff and whole-system assessments that do not undermine good practice but build upon it*
- *enjoy a culture of listening based upon empathetic understanding and a willingness to appreciate the view of the other*
- *teach pupils some knowledge of how the brain works so that they understand we are wired for compassion*
- *allow its pupils and staff the space to contemplate, to reflect, to be mindful*

- *be proactive in its local and wider community*
- *be proactive in building local, national and international cohesion*
- *be a health-promoting school that pays due regard to the social, emotional and spiritual aspect of learning*
- *be a school that really values educating the heart*
- *be a school that is culturally inclusive and meets the needs of its diverse pupil population*
- *be a school that safeguards its pupils and teaches them skills to live in this digital age*
- *practice restorative justice as part of its behaviour policy*
- *be a school that balances high attainment with self-esteem*
- *be a campaigning school, championing the rights of others and the needs of the planet*
- *celebrate and regularly praise kindness and compassionate acts*
- *encourage the ideal of service, collegiality and love in action for our global interconnected universe*
- *be a happy school with lots of smiling faces.*[28]

We can sum up the characteristics of the compassionate educator and the compassionate school as 'love in action'. The adoption of this principle in everything we do in school life provides the Golden Thread through which we help young people create a better and more just world. Students must still attain, must develop academic, vocational, and social skills, but should have a more balanced purpose of elevating service, rather than self, as the key virtue. If pupils leave our care celebrating the maxim that 'universal compassion is the only guarantee of morality' (Schopenhauer, cited in Dossey, 2013:6), we will have gone some way to fulfilling our responsibilities to future generations. I end with the words of St. Paul (from one of the greatest short tracts ever written) who, in response to the Christian Corinthians' question as to who was the greatest God, argues, simply, that it was Love:

If I speak in the tongues of mortals and of angels, but do not have love, I am a noisy gong or a clanging cymbal. And if I have prophetic powers, and understand all mysteries and all knowledge, and if I have all faith, so as to remove mountains, but do not have love, I am nothing. If I give away all my possession, and if I hand over my body so that I may boast, but do not have love, I gain nothing.

Love is patient; love is kind; love is not envious or boastful or arrogant or rude. It does not insist on its own way; it is not irritable or resentful; it bears all things, believes all things, hopes all things, and endures all things.

Love never ends. But as for prophecies, they will come to an end; as for tongues, they will cease; as for knowledge, it will pass away. When I was a child, I spoke like a child, I thought like a child, I reasoned like a child; when I became an adult, I put an end to childish ways. And now faith, hope, and love abide, these three; and the greatest of these is love. (1 Corinthians, Chapter 3: 1-13) [98]

17–30 YEARS

HOW DO I LOVE THEE?

How do I love thee? Let me count the ways.
I love thee to the depth and breadth and height
My soul can reach, when feeling out of sight
For the ends of being and ideal grace.
I love thee to the level of every day's
Most quiet need, by sun and candle-light.
I love thee freely, as men strive for right.
I love thee purely, as they turn from praise.
I love thee with the passion put to use
In my old griefs, and with my childhood's faith.
I love thee with a love I seemed to lose
With my lost saints. I love thee with the breath,
Smiles, tears, of all my life; and, if God choose,
I shall but love thee better after death.

Elizabeth Barrett Browning [30]

Care, Concern and Compassion in Higher Education

There is no getting away from the fact that the primary task of a university is to deliver educational programmes that will ensure the students are:

1. Fit for the award (BSc/MA/PhD)
2. Fit to practice their chosen profession (to meet the appropriate professional standards)
3. Fit for purpose

I will elaborate on the concept of "fit for purpose" in the next stage (30-65 years).

Education is a *relational practice.* As faculty exercise their judgement, and offer their skills and expertise, individually and in teams, they are always in relationship with their students and each other. The quality of their work, the experience of students, and the effectiveness and efficiency of their efforts depend on the quality of these relationships. These relationships need to be supported and sustained by *healthy relational systems.*

Faculty and administrative staff work within human service organisations and not supermarkets or factories. Healthy relational systems are about more than just targets, procedures, and structures. They are about embedding care into every level of the organisation and every student contact.

When there is pressure for efficiency, for the effective organisation of services, for meeting targets, for answering to regulators, these systems can be dominated by concerns and approaches that actively undermine the relational nature of the work.

Building a healthy relational system begins by recognising the costly emotional work required for the student to leave his/her alma mater – fit for purpose.

Students arriving at their university are leaving, or have left, the familiar family setting and place. Attachment behaviour in this instance should be regarded as a normal and healthy part of one's instinctive make up. It is most misleading to term it regressive or childish when seen in an adult (student).

Alma Mater Studiorum

Alma mater studiorum, or "nurturing mother of studies", was chosen by the oldest university in the western world (Bologna, founded 1088) as their motto on its crest. Many other universities have since adopted the motto. It is, however, more often than not, used to refer to the university one has attended, ie. "my alma mater", when one does not know its derivation or true meaning. The name "Alma" itself has the masculine version "Almo". Both are often translated as meaning "feeds one soul" or "lifts the spirits". Alma mater studiorum is taken to mean the "nurturing mother of studies".

The concept of alma mater studiorum – "the nurturing mother of studies" – can act as an overarching guide for faculty and staff to provide the necessary environment to enable students to meet their learning needs and to become "fit for purpose".

In-house training for faculty and staff should be a requirement so they can recognise the models of attachment behaviour as identified and described by Bowlby and his followers.

If a university is to act as a "mother" to its students (and faculty) then it needs to operate in ways that create positive and effective "attachments".

The mentoring programme a university espouses to become an alma mater studiorum needs to offer more than a tutorial or supervision or appraisal. It should be confidential and take place outside the managerial framework of the organisation. It occurs in addition to all the more formal activities that are available. Mentoring will allow the student to address the critique of current university teaching as outlined by Donald Schon in his seminal paper "The Crisis of Professional Knowledge and the Pursuit of an Epistemology of Practice".[31]

Schon's work has attracted much attention to his concept of the "reflective practitioner" which is applicable in every area of professional activity. Schon calls for the liberation of the professions from the tyranny of the university-based professional schools; he is criticising the influence of misplaced "scientific" methodologies. In Schon's view, the university-based professional schools have succumbed to the erroneous view that good professional practice is dependent on the use of "describable, testable, replicable techniques derived from scientific research based on knowledge that is objective, consensual, cumulative, and convergent". His different perspective that involves practitioners "making judgements of quality for which they cannot state adequate criteria or displaying skills for which they cannot describe procedures or rules" evokes, as Vickers[32] did, the importance of tacit knowledge. Schon argues that tacit areas of knowledge or skill form some of the most important aspects of competent practice. He terms the differing approaches to the professional task as those of "rigour or relevance". Schon's book *The Reflective*

Practitioner: How Professionals Think in Action [33] published in 1983 provides us with a programme of change which has had, as yet, little impact on university education generally.

The mentoring will provide the student an opportunity to engage in numerous reflection/action cycles that will lead to his own ability to manage the life-long learning that will be required if he is to be fit for purpose.

Training should be offered to post-graduate students to act as mentors to their undergraduate colleagues.

Mentoring Programme – A Working Definition [34]

Personal support in the context of continuing education and professional development.

Key Concepts

- Addressing current professional concerns.
- Providing space and time to reflect on and evaluate the professional task.
- Offering help with career appraisal and development.
- Exploring the professional personal/boundary.
- Mentoring is a confidential relationship.

Steward and Stewardship

Steward:	A twelfth century Old English word used to describe someone employed to "manage", or "look after" a large household.
Stewardship:	Many theological and religious meanings – links to the Bible and the concept of the Good Shepherd.
Steward and Stewardship	Now in common use referring to environmental concerns. Responsible use and protection of the natural environment through conservation and sustainable practices.

Professor Mike Thomas when Vice-Chancellor of the University of Central Lancashire (UCLan) highlighted the challenges faced by organisational leaders who have the desire to influence changes within large organisations. He wrote in a recent article in the Higher Education Supplement entitled "Heroic Leadership is a Campus Villain". [35]

Universities are not capitalist enterprises, and leaders forget this at their peril. Business models purloined from the private sector will always be an uneasy fit. We occupy a distinctive position in society, straddling elements of the private, public and charitable spheres.

So rather than the heroic model, I'm an advocate of the "stewardship model". University leaders are "keepers of the flame", custodians of institutions that are more important than any one individual. During our tenure, we are charged with ensuring that our institutions continue to succeed in their remits to offer people the life-changing benefits of higher education and enable them to achieve their potential. These values are important because they provide the foundation of our activities.

Stewardship and Leadership – a Whole University Approach

Professor Mark Dooris and his colleagues have published a most scholarly and substantial report, "Healthy Universities: Whole University Leadership for Health, Wellbeing and Sustainability". [36] This report is co-authored and chaired by Professor Mark Dooris, Dr. Alan Farrier from UCLan and Professor Sue Powell from Manchester Metropolitan University. The report builds on the 2015 Okanagan Charter[37] and will provide all who are involved in this work the framework to implement the detailed recommendations and conclusions.

Recommendations for senior level leaders

- Make a commitment to health and wellbeing a key strategic priority, acknowledging that this underpins core university business and productivity.
- Adopt a whole university approach. This means focusing on the entire university community; appreciating that health has multiple determinants and consequences embedding this commitment within and across all areas and activities; and connecting across boundaries.
- Ensure that action to protect and promote health and wellbeing is effectively jointed up with parallel agendas such as sustainability, resilience and equality and diversity.

- Balance top-down commitment to health and well-being with a distributed leadership model that embeds this commitment into multiple roles and responsibilities.
- Complement strategic leadership with a process of cultural change-building, wide-ranging ownership, and shifting mindsets among staff and students.
- Enable the development and coordination of the Healthy University through resourcing a dedicated post or team.
- Align whole university approaches advocated by different strategic agendas and respond to high-profile issues (e.g. mental health) within the context of a wider healthy universities' commitment to health, wellbeing, and sustainability.

So how does compassion fit into a university curriculum? I am often asked this question, and I very rarely have the opportunity to answer it as I would like to, but I will now:

1. If I am asked by a theologian or someone of faith, I would mention the Golden Rule,[38] as identified by major world religions, and that compassion is among the highest of human virtues.
2. If I am asked by a psychologist, I would mention words like altruism, empathy and kindness.
3. If I were asked by an anthropologist, I would mention pro-social behaviour and imprinting á la Konrad Lorenz.[39]
4. If I were asked by a sociologist, I would point him to Marmot and Wilkinson's breath-taking work on *Social Determinants of Health: The Solid Facts*[40] and Wilkinson and Pickett's [41] work on income inequality and its impact on mental health.

5. If I were asked by a member of my own discipline – medicine or public health, I would say we have lost the plot and we no longer link disease, illness and sickness in our understanding of what health care should be all about.

6. If I were asked by a modern Darwinist, I would mention competitive/collaborative nature of our genepool and the epigenetic impact of our environment. I would also add how the exhibition of compassion influences our mate selection.

7. If I were asked by a neuroscientist, I would talk about the evolution of the triune brain and the importance of norepinephrine and the vagus nerve.

8. If I were asked by a businessman, I would talk about game theory and the level of adrenaline identified in stockbrokers and hedge fund managers.

9. If I were asked by an ecologist, I would outline the relationship the Anthropocene has had over the last eight thousand years, but particularly in the last one thousand years on our ecosystem that we are rapidly destroying.

10. If I were asked by an educationist I would mention the work done in some schools now with helping our young children learning the value of diaphragmatic breathing and meditation (mindfulness).

11. If I were asked by a language and literature teacher, I would point to how reading selected poetry can allow and facilitate the emergence of compassion as a feeling.

Summing up

A poem (extract), a quote, a diagram and a challenge.

1. Poem

    To see a World in a Grain of Sand
    And a Heaven in a Wild Flower
    Hold Infinity in the palm of your hand
    And Eternity in an hour

    "Auguries of Innocence" – W Blake [42]

2. Quote

    Only connect the prose and passion, and both will
    be exalted, and human love will be seen at its height.
    Live in fragments no longer.

    Howard's End – E M Forster [43]

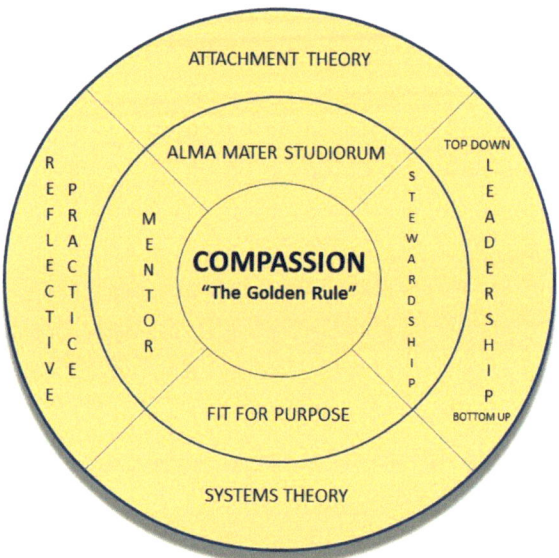

Unless we restore the concept of compassion (The Golden Rule) as the binding ingredient within our educational system, we will continue to ensure our students leave our universities not fit for purpose for the challenges they will face whatever their future careers may be.

30–65 YEARS

THE ROAD NOT TAKEN

Two roads diverged in a yellow wood,
And sorry I could not travel both
And be one traveler, long I stood
And looked down one as far as I could
To where it bent in the undergrowth;

Then took the other, as just as fair,
And having perhaps the better claim,
Because it was grassy and wanted wear;
Though as for that the passing there
Had worn them really about the same,

And both that morning equally lay
In leaves no step had trodden black.
Oh, I kept the first for another day!
Yet knowing how way leads on to way,
I doubted if I should ever come back.

I shall be telling this with a sigh
Somewhere ages and ages hence:
Two roads diverged in a wood, and I—
I took the one less traveled by,
And that has made all the difference.

Robert Frost [44]

Fit for Purpose – Life-long Learning

Much could be written, and indeed, much has been written concerning these two concepts. A very brief description of what these principles address is the difference between TRAINING and EDUCATION.

Training prepares the student for the known.
Education prepares the student for the unknown.

The major critique for university education is that it has increasingly confused the former with the latter. Universities have been turned into "businesses" where the excellence of the "teaching" is measured by the subsequent salary potential obtained by the student. The commodification of modules and courses and the closed windows and/or the silo-mentality of the different academic disciplines does not prepare the graduate to become fit for purpose.

To become "fit for purpose", the graduate of the university will need to continue with a programme of life-long learning. As Kolb describes "knowledge results from the combination of grasping and transforming experience".[45] Kolb helped to identify students' "learning styles" which had major implications for what has become known as experiential learning theory (ELT).

Like Schon, Vickers and others, Kolb identified the contrast between teacher-centred and learner-centred education – the latter ensuring the student leaves university with the motivation and skill set to become a life-long learner.

Where does compassion fit into this educational theory? In the position paper we wrote at the launching conference of the Darwin International Institute for the Study of Compassion (DIISC),[46] we noted an academic saying that, "It is impossible to say everything that can be said about a topic". This is certainly true about the academic study of compassion.

Easily championed, but everywhere alarmingly challenged, compassion can too readily be relegated to a "soft" or "pious" quality, side-lined by more instrumental, technical, pragmatic or ideological concerns. Compassion needs to be re-considered, re-evaluated and integrated into the understanding and practices of society as:

- a primary value and requirement in a modern world, which at individual, social, institutional, and political levels frequently fosters its opposite – to the extent that fear of annihilation of valued social institutions, of groups, and of the self – is widespread;
- treating the other(s) with the same concern, attention and generosity that one would wish for oneself; refraining from treating them as one would not wish for oneself; being open to, disturbed by, sympathetic to, and moved to respond to the experience and pain of others;
- a difficult and challenging quality that itself requires better understanding; which also requires the recognition of, and engagement with, pain, damage, anxiety, anger, and difference, and the exploitative, competitive, violent or simply self-centred feelings and motives by which human beings, individually and collectively, are also driven;

- something that has been split off from and relegated to a subsidiary place in technical or professional skills, and collective enterprises, and that needs to be reintegrated as a core and primary component of all such practices and wider social relations;
- an evolutionary phenomenon emerging as a positive and dynamic aspect in social relations as human beings have learned to cooperate and preserve themselves and their communities;
- an attitude and a practice that, in turn, depends on social relations for its cultivation and sustenance. Such relations can be thought about, constructed, and nourished to do that, or conversely can work directly against compassionate mindedness and behaviour;
- a quality that depends on the individual, the group, the organisation and society developing the skills and the habit of self-awareness and reflection;
- a quality that requires a dialogue for its exploration and understanding. This would allow for synthesis between the following discourses: scientific, psychological, philosophical, historical, cultural, religious, sociological, and political perspectives.

65–90 YEARS

AFTERWARDS

When the Present has latched its postern behind my tremulous stay,
And the May month flaps its glad green leaves like wings,
Delicate-filmed as new-spun silk, will the neighbours say,
'He was a man who used to notice such things'?

If it be in the dusk when, like an eyelid's soundless blink,
The dewfall-hawk comes crossing the shades to alight
Upon the wind-warped upland thorn, a gazer may think,
'To him this must have been a familiar sight.'

If I pass during some nocturnal blackness, mothy and warm,
When the hedgehog travels furtively over the lawn,
One may say,
    'He strove that such innocent creatures should come to no harm,
But he could do little for them; and now he is gone.'

If, when hearing that I have been stilled at last, they stand at the door,
Watching the full-starred heavens that winter sees
Will this thought rise on those who will meet my face no more,
'He was one who had an eye for such mysteries'?

And will any say when my bell of quittance is heard in the gloom
And a crossing breeze cuts a pause in its outrollings,
Till they rise again, as they were a new bell's boom,
'He hears it not now, but used to notice such things'?

Thomas Hardy [47]

Education in the Third Age (Retirement)

This label refers to the first age of education (5–25), the second age of work (25–65) and the third age of retirement (65 –). Some writers now challenge the linear sequential timing of these three stages. Many now start work and then return to education, some "retire" early then resume work and or education. What we are exploring in this section is the focus on adult learners past 60/65 who return back to formal or informal educational activities to address several different needs. Some countries have established universities specifically targeted to this age group. However, more often than not individuals will seek to attend courses to learn a special skill in IT or cooking or drama without the need or wish to obtain a formal certificate or an award. Some do go on and take a full-time education course leading to a Bachelors/Masters or indeed a PhD. Others will undertake less educationally focussed activities and join a dance group, a painting class, or a walking group. More often than not, many of the courses are undertaken online. Surveys suggest that part of the reason for undertaking these activities is driven by a wish to meet and socialise, often as a result of the death of a long-term partner. Personally, I prefer to envelope "education in the third age" within the concept of "life-long learning". There is no reason to separate out this stage of our lives and label it "retirement". The language we use – "old age", "senior citizen", "geriatric", "old folk", or "past it" demeans and categorises this stage of life in a negative way. Many cultures revere and respect "the elders" of their society and will see them as a resource of wisdom and security.

Learning can no longer be dichotomized into a place and time to acquire knowledge (school) and a place and

time to apply the knowledge acquired (the workplace).[48]
*Instead, learning can be seen as something that takes place
on an ongoing basis from our daily interactions with others
and with the world around us. It can create and shapeshift into
the form of formal learning or informal learning, or self-
directed learning. Allen Tough (1979), Canadian educator
and researcher, asserts that almost 70% of learning projects
are self-planned.*[49]

So do not wait until you retire or reach 60 or 65 to take up
"education in the third age".

Life-long learning is distinguished from the concept of continuing
education in the sense that it has a broader scope. Unlike the
latter, which is oriented towards adult education, developed for
the needs of schools and industries, this type of learning is con-
cerned with the development of human potential, recognising
each individual's capacity for it. [50]

Life-long learning will ensure that when you do reach the age
of retirement, you will avoid Shakespeare's somewhat negative
description of the "last scene of all".

> *… Last scene of all,*
> *That ends this strange eventful history,*
> *Is second childishness and mere oblivion;*
> *Sans teeth, sans eyes, sans taste, sans everything.* [51]

The prize for adopting a life-long learning approach from an
early age is that it will enable you to want to continue to learn
when, supposedly, you have retired. The chances of developing

Alzheimer's will be much reduced, and you may find that you have stumbled on what others might label as wisdom.

Compassion and wisdom are interconnected. Wisdom drives you to be compassionate and compassionate actions are the building blocks for wisdom.

References

1. Pietroni, P. (2020). *Sounds, Music, Gazing and Touch.* Unpublished.
2. Darwin, C. (1871). *The Descent of Man,* and *Selection in Relation to Sex.* London. John Murray.
3. Darwin, C. *ibid.*
4. Higgins, R. (1978). *The Seventh Enemy; the Human Factor in the Global Crisis.* New York. McGraw-Hill.
5. Barks, C. (1995). *The Essential Rumi.* Harper Collins. New York.
6. Armstrong, K. (2008). *My wish: the Charter for Compassion.* Available at www.ted.com/speakers/karen_armstrong (last accessed April 2020).
7. Summerhill. Available at www.summerhillschool.co.uk/ (last accessed April 2020).
8. Montessori, M. Available at https://www.biography.com/scholar/maria-montessori (last accessed April 2020).
9. The Open University. Available at (last accessed April 2020).
10. Shakespeare, W. *As You Like It, Act II, Scene VII (All the world's a stage).* Available at https://www.poetryfoundation.org/poems/56966/speech-all-the-worlds-a-stage (last accessed April 2020).
11. Bowlby, J (1988). *Attachment and Loss* series: *Attachment; Separation: Anxiety and Anger;* and *Loss: Sadness and Depression.* Tavistock Professional Book. London. Routledge.
12. Coles, M. I. (Ed.). (2015). *Towards the Compassionate School: from Golden Rule to Golden Thread.* London. UCL Institute of Education Press.

13. Intrator, S. M., & Scribner, M. (Eds.). (2014). *Teaching with Heart.* San Francisco. Jossey-Bass.

14. Waddington, K. (Ed.) (Forthcoming, 2021). *Towards the Compassionate University: From Golden Thread to Global Impact.* Abingdon New York. Routledge.

15. Aguilar, E. (2013). *Five Reasons Why We Need Poetry in Schools.* Available at www.edutopia.org/blog/five-reasons-poetry-needed-schools-elena-aguilar(last accessed April 2020).

16. *The Poet Warriors Project.* Available at http://poetwarriorsproject.com/ (last accessed April 2020).

17. Parker, S. (2014). *Take Part.* Well Versed: Why Teaching Poetry Matters. Available at (last accessed April 2020).

18. Sheridan, M. L. (2006). *I Never Knew.* Available at https://www.familyfriendpoems.com/poem/my-daughter-my-love (last accessed April 2020).

19. Beichman, A., Martino, A., & Minogue, K. (1982) *Three Myths*, The Heritage Lectures, (Washington) 7.

20. Bowlby, J (1988). op. cit.

21. Bowlby, J. (2000. First published 1979). *The Making and Breaking of Affectional Bonds.* London. Routledge.

22. Bowlby, J. (2003. First published 1988). *A Secure Base: Clinical Application of Attachment Theory.* Hove. Brunner-Routledge.

23. Bowlby, J. (1991). *Charles Darwin: A New Life.* New York: Norton.

24. Bowlby, J. (2000. First published 1979). op. cit.

25. Bowlby, J. (2000. First published 1979). op. cit.

26. Erskine, R. (1998). The Therapeutic Relationship: Integrating Motivation and Personality Theories. *Transactional Analysis Journal,* April 1998. Available at https://www.researchgate.net/publication/258191060_The_Therapeutic_Relationship_Integrating_Motivation_and_Personality_Theories (last accessed April 2020).

27. Kipling, R. (1943). *A choice of Kipling's Verse made by T.S. Eliot.* If. London. Faber and Faber. Available at www.poetryfoundation.org/poems/46473/if--- (last accessed April 2020).

28. Coles, M. I. (Ed.). ibid.

29. Coles, M. I. (Ed.). ibid.

30. Browning, E. B. (1850). *How Do I love Thee? (Sonnet 43).* Available at https://poets.org/poem/how-do-i-love-thee-sonnet-43

(last accessed April 2020).

31. Schon, D. (1987). The Crisis of Professional Knowledge and the Pursuit of an Epistemology of Practice. Delivered at Harvard Business School 75th Anniversary Colloquium on Teaching by the Case Method. Open University Press 52. Reprinted in *Journal of Interprofessional Care,* 6(1): pp 49-63 (1992).

32. Vickers, G. (1983). *Human Systems are Different.* London: Harper & Row.

33. Schon, D. (1983). *The Reflective Practitioner: How Professionals Think in Action.* New York: Basic Books. Available at www.daneshnamehicsa.ir/userfiles/file/Manabeh? The%20Reflective%20Practitioner%20(2).pdf (last accessed April 2020).

34. The Elizabeth Bryan Foundation Trust (2016). Available at: www.ebft.org.uk. (last accessed November 2019).

35. Thomas, M. (2018). *Heroic Leadership is a Campus Villain.* Available at www.timeshighereducation.com/opinion/heroic-leadership-campus-villain (last accessed April 2020).

36. Dooris, M., Farrier, A. & Powell, S. (2018). *Healthy Universities: whole university leadership for health, wellbeing and sustainability.* Available at www.lfhe.ac.uk/en/ research-resources/publications-hub/index.cfm/SDP2017UCLAN (last accessed: April 2020).

37. International Conference on Health Promoting Universities and Colleges (2015). *Okanagan Charter: An International Charter for Health Promoting Universities and Colleges.* Wilkinson, R.G. & Pickett, K.E. (2010). *The Spirit Level. Why Equality is Better for Everyone.* London: Penguin.

38. The Golden Rule. Available at https://charterforcompassion.org/share-the-charter/compassion-and-the-real-meaning-of-the-golden-rule (last accessed April 2020).

39. Konrad Lorenz. Available at www.britannica.com/biography/ Kodrad-Lorenz (last accessed April 2020).

40. World Health Organization. (2nd Ed. 2003). *Social Determinants of Health: The Solid Facts.* Wilkinson, R. G. & Marmot, M. (Eds.).

41. Wilkinson, R.G. & Pickett, K.E. (2010). *The Spirit Level. Why Equality is Better for Everyone.* London: Penguin.

42. Blake, W. (1863). *Auguries of Innocence.*

Available at www.poetryfoundation.org/poems/43650/auguries-of-innocence (last accessed April 2020).

43. Forster, E.M. (1991). First published 1910). *Howards End*. London. David Campbell Publishers.

44. Frost, R. (1916). *The Road Not Taken*.
Available at https://poetryfoundation/org/poems/44272/the-road-not-taken (last accessed April 2020).

45. Kolb, D.A. (1984). *Experiential learning: experience as the source of learning and development*. New Jersey. Prentice-Hall. Available at www.researchgate.net/publication/235701029_Experiential_Learning_Experience_As_The_Source_Of_Learning_and_Development (last accessed April 2020).

46. Darwin International Institute for the Study of Compassion. Available at https://diisc.org/dct (last accessed April 2020).

47. Hardy, T (1917) *Afterwards*. Available at https://www.poemhunter.com/poem/afterwards/ (last accessed April 2020).

48. Fischer, G. (2000). Lifelong Learning – More than Training. *Journal of Interactive Learning Research*. Vol. 11, No. 3/4.

49. Tough, A. M. (1979). *The Adult's Learning Projects: A Fresh Approach to Theory and Practice in Adult Learning*. Michigan. Ontario Institute for Studies in Education.

50. Longworth, N. & Davies, W. K. (2013. First published 1996). *Lifelong Learning*. Oxon. Routledge.

51. Shakespeare, W. ibid.

Photo Credits

www.waymarking.com/gallery/image.aspx?f=1&guid=f5c04f6e-1ff3-438b-9802-023c1f814911, p. 10
Guillaume de Germain, p. 14
Nikhita S, p. 21
Shutterstock, p. 29
Shutterstock, p. 41
Tim Mossholder, p. 46

Publisher
SF Design, llc / Fresco Books
Albuquerque, New Mexico
frescobooks.com

ISBN: 978-1-934491-77-5